MW00578579

Presented to

_____

By

_____

On the Occasion of

_____

Date

_____

THE
PRAYER
for
ABUNDANT
FAVOR

Clarence L. Blasier

Matthew Publishing Company
North Canton, Ohio

© 2002 by Clarence L. Blasier

Cover design by Veda Harris

ISBN 0-9625444-9-3

All Scripture is taken from the King James Version of the Bible.

Published by Matthew Publishing Company
717 S. Main Street, North Canton, OH 44720

Printed in the United States of America

THE
PRAYER
for
ABUNDANT
FAVOR

CONTENTS

PREFACE

Be assured that what you are about to read is neither another "name it and claim it" book nor one that depicts God as a genie in a bottle, whose sole desire is to grant your every wish. *The Prayer for Abundant Favor* is one that recognizes that God is fully in control, and that we should confess our weaknesses and inability to accomplish any meaningful thing without God's hand being in it. This prayer should be prayed with a humble heart filled with gratitude for God's concern for our needs.

Mercy, grace, and favor are granted at God's discretion, and not because we *merit* them or are *entitled* to them. It is because God loves us that He *chooses* to bless us. As we approach the *throne of grace* for any reason, the words of Exodus 33:18,19 ring loud and clear.

"And he [Moses] said, I beseech thee, show me thy glory.

And he [God] said, I will make all my goodness pass before thee, and I will proclaim the name of the Lord before thee; <u>and will be gracious to whom I will be gracious, and will show mercy on whom I will show mercy</u>."   (underlining mine)

The fact that, as a Christian, I am a child of God, an heir to His kingdom, and a joint heir with Christ (Romans 8:16,17) does not relieve me of responsibility nor does it obligate God to show me any special favor. When He does so it is because of His perfect love, to accomplish His purposes and for His name's sake. My needs and desires are important to God, but His sovereignty is above all. With these thoughts established, we can look with greater clarity at *The Prayer for Abundant Favor.*

Clarence L. Blasier

PART I

GOD'S
FAVOR EXAMINED

THE PREDICAMENT

For most people, preparing for a meeting with the much feared Internal Revenue Service can be more than traumatic to say the least—especially when you know their claim against you is in the thousands of dollars. You cannot help but assume they are prepared to take any action necessary to get their money. It doesn't matter who is right or who is wrong, they have the upper hand. You spend sleepless nights and anxious hours, and live in fear of the outcome—*that is, if you have never learned to pray for God's favor.*

This is the position I found myself in about twenty years ago. I had made a large investment that afforded excellent tax advantages. However, due to what apparently was a change in the position the IRS was taking on certain types of tax shelter programs, the tax benefits were disallowed.

Upon bad advice from my attorney, I foolishly let the matter ride with the intention of contesting it in court if necessary. Belatedly, my attorney learned that in similar cases the courts were ruling in favor of the IRS. Therefore, we did not proceed in that direction and I found myself deeply indebted, not only for the tax savings on the original deduction, but for thousands of additional dollars in penalties and interest.

There was no way I could even begin to pay the amount involved, but I knew they would try to recover what they could. It should have been a time of desperation, anxiety, self-incrimination, uncertainty, and fear—and it was—*until I learned how to pray for God's abundant favor*!

HELP IS ON THE WAY

Several days prior to the IRS meeting, for some reason, the name of Nick came to mind. I had admired his solid Christian witness for some time and knew that he was what is called a prayer warrior. So I phoned, and without giving him too many details, explained that I needed his prayer support and would like to have lunch with him to discuss the reason. He readily agreed and we made plans to meet the following day.

I arrived at the restaurant at noon expecting to find Nick inside at a table. But there he was, waiting at the entrance. He came to the car and informed me that a friend of his, Bill, had called, and after hearing the purpose of our get-together, had asked if he could join us. Would I mind? Of course I wouldn't, but I could not help but question how freely I could discuss my problem with a stranger present.

I must tell you that, as I look back, I realize that of His own choosing, God's hand was in all this. It was God, through the Holy Spirit, who brought Nick's name to mind. It was the Holy Spirit who moved Nick's friend to call. It was God who changed our luncheon plans. And it was God who brought about all that followed at that time and all that has transpired since.

You must also know that between the time of the investment and the ruling by the IRS, I had asked Jesus Christ to become Lord of my life. Like so many, I was saved at an early age but had never fully committed myself to Him. I mention this because I certainly had done nothing to be worthy of God's favor—in fact, I wasn't even walking as a child of His should be walking. But praise God, through His grace and all that occurred, I learned what is available to every child of God. I learned about His favor and how to receive it.

NICK, BILL, AND I

Nick, his friend, and I enjoyed the lunch immensely. As it turned out, Bill was very knowledgeable about praying for God's favor. After he understood my situation, he shared his knowledge with us along with some of his personal experiences. It was an exciting time as we learned more about God's love and grace and how He bestows it upon His children. Of course, Bill also led us in prayer, seeking God's favor for me with the IRS in the upcoming meeting.

PREPARATION AND MEETING

From the time of the luncheon until I faced the IRS agent, I continued to pray daily for God's favor, as did Nick and his friend. God immediately gave me peace of mind. But He did much more than that. When the time for the meeting came, I arrived with complete confidence that God had gone before me and prepared the heart of the person I was to meet. My attorney's young associate accompanied me, but he never said a word—and none was needed.

Even with all the prayer preparation, what occurred at the meeting came as a complete surprise. Rather than being confrontational as one would normally expect, the IRS agent spent the entire time showing me in a friendly manner how I could resolve the problem with a special settlement. Obviously, I followed his advice. It took time and it wasn't the easiest process in the world, but the debt was eliminated, thanks to God hearing and answering our prayers. God had truly granted me His special favor with a person I had never met and have not seen since. But that's only the beginning.

MORE FAVOR GRACE UPON GRACE

In the years since the events already described, not only has God answered my personal prayers for favor numerous times, but He has also answered the prayers of many others with whom I have had the privilege of sharing this blessed hope.

MY FRIEND NEAL

Neal is a close friend who was in what appeared to be a no-win situation. He and his partner were engaged in building homes on a small scale. They had purchased a choice lot for a single dwelling, but there was a problem. Because of the water drainage pattern, they were unable to obtain a building permit. Week after week they argued and pleaded, but to no avail. The city engineer would not budge. In fact, he curtly informed them that he would never issue a permit for that site. However, he had never heard of how God answers His childrens' prayers for favor.

A LIGHT AT THE END OF THE TUNNEL

I first learned about Neal's problem during a weekend retreat sponsored by our church. We stayed together in the same cabin and during one of our conversations, Neal explained his dilemma. Now I was able to share my knowledge and experiences just as Bill had done with me. After thoroughly discussing the concept of God's favor, we prayed together.

On Monday morning Neal walked into the office of the engineer, whose first words were, "Where's that paper you want me to sign?" Does Neal believe God hears and answers prayers for favor? You bet he does!

FAVOR WITH RON

Ron had been in the hospital for nearly three months suffering from leukemia and other serious complications when his mother asked me to visit him. From my conversation with her, I knew of his attitude toward "religion," the Bible, and people who witness for the Lord. I was naturally apprehensive about the reception I would receive, but again, God was faithful.

Before the visit, I prayed and asked God to open Ron's heart to the truth and to grant me favor in his eyes. During the first visit, as we became acquainted I was able to briefly but freely discuss the free gift of salvation that was available to him. On the second visit, Ron accepted Christ as his personal Savior. He is growing spiritually and his leukemia is in remission.

By far, the best reason we can ever have for asking God's favor is to lead another person to Christ—to further His work and His kingdom.

GOD'S FAVOR

For purposes of our discussion, when it involves relationships between people, let's describe *favor* as *goodwill*. When we are in a person's favor, we are experiencing their *goodwill* which can be manifested in many ways. When we are in God's favor, His *goodwill* is conferred upon us. It is a precious gift from an Almighty God.

We have strongly emphasized that God is sovereign and bestows His favor at His discretion and upon whomever He chooses. God also may withhold His favor at His discretion from whomever He chooses. We are not *entitled* to this favor. It is given because of our heavenly Father's love and compassion for us and for whatever other reasons only He knows.

I believe that, according to the Scriptures, there are two types of favor. The first is **inherent** with being a child of God and in a right relationship with Him. As a result of years of personal experience and much biblical research, I believe there also are times when God bestows special or ***abundant favor*** either directly to or on behalf of His children. But my opinion is of little or no importance. Let's look at what the Bible has to say.

INHERENT FAVOR

You have no doubt heard the rather humorous expression that describes the word *inherent* fairly well. When someone in business is promoted to a high position such as vice president of a bank, you may have heard the statement, *"Now he gets his own parking space and a key to the men's room."* These privileges are *inherent* with the position to which the man has been appointed. They go with it. But in considering the *inherent favor* that God gives, a familiar passage from the Psalms offers a much better explanation:

"For thou, Lord, wilt bless the righteous; with favor wilt thou compass [crown] him as with a shield."
(Psalm 5:12)

This verse says that *the righteous* will be blessed with favor. Now we know that any righteousness we have is not of ourselves, but of God. If, and only if, we have become a child of God by accepting Jesus Christ as our personal Savior and have been forgiven of our sins, then in God's eyes we are righteous. But remember, it is *God's* righteousness imputed to us that makes us righteous in His sight. (*See* Romans 4; Philippians 3:6-9.)

Proverbs 14:9 tells us, "...*Among the righteous there is favor.*"

Now do you see why I believe that *God's favor* (*goodwill*) is *inherent* with becoming a Christian and a child of God? It's simply because God's Word tells us so. The bank vice president may have received his prestigious parking space and his key, but we receive much, much more. Earthly blessings and privileges can never be compared to those God offers. If our relationship with Him is right, then moment by moment and day by day, we walk in His *goodwill—His favor*. This knowledge alone gives us greater confidence in our status as an adopted child of God and in His continual presence within us.

However, the knowledge that we walk in God's favor should never cause us to be arrogant. The opposite is true. When we consider that **Almighty God—the Creator, the One who is Love, the Great I AM**—would deign to show us His favor, it should be a cause for much humility and deep gratitude.

The question: "If we already have God's *inherent favor*, how can we be sure that there is added favor...*abundant favor?*" Answer: As before, the Bible tells us so.

ABUNDANT FAVOR

Abundant favor, as used here, can be defined as unusual favor, or favor that is out of the ordinary. It is an added measure of favor. Jesus said that He came to this earth that we "might have life, and have it more abundantly." God is most anxious to grant many blessings to His children and abundant favor is one of them.

There are numerous instances where special favor, or *abundant favor*, was granted to people God chose. Bear in mind, though, that those to whom *abundant favor* was granted also walked in *inherent favor*. They knew God—He knew them.

JOSEPH AND ABUNDANT FAVOR

One of the early recorded examples of abundant favor is that of Joseph, the young man with the coat of many colors. As you recall, Joseph's brothers hated him and had plotted to kill him, but one of them (Reuben) intervened and instead Joseph was thrown into a pit to be abandoned. However, in a short time a group of traders on their way to Egypt appeared and the brothers decided to sell Joseph to them for twenty pieces of silver. When once in Egypt, the traders sold Joseph (at a profit, I'm sure) to Potiphar, an officer of Pharaoh and captain of the guard. Genesis 39 says that the Lord was with Joseph and he found grace (abundant favor) in the eyes of his master who made him overseer over his house and all his possessions.

The Bible tells us that the Lord blessed the Egyptian's house and all his fields. Joseph was highly successful and admired by all, but there was trouble afoot. Potiphar's wife lusted after Joseph and begged him to lie with her. When he refused, she falsely accused him of attacking her. Potiphar was incensed, especially after all that he had done for Joseph, and commanded that Joseph be put in prison.

"But the Lord was with Joseph, and showed him mercy and gave him favor [abundant favor] in the sight of the keeper of the prison." (Genesis 39:21)

Again, by God's hand, Joseph received special favor in the eyes of the jailer and he was placed in charge of all the other prisoners.

GOD'S PURPOSE REVEALED

As the story unfolds, we understand more about God's purpose in continuing to grant Joseph abundant favor.

One of the reasons Joseph's brothers had hated him was because God had given him the ability to interpret dreams. Pharaoh was desperate to find a person who could interpret several of his dreams as none of the magicians and wise men of his kingdom could do so. When Joseph's ability was disclosed to Pharaoh, Joseph was summoned. He accurately described and interpreted each dream. They foretold seven years of bountiful harvest for the land of Egypt followed by seven years of severe drought. His recommendation to Pharaoh was that one-fifth of the harvest be set aside during the seven plentiful years to supply food during the lean years. And who was placed in charge of this plan? Joseph!

Not only was Joseph given the authority to implement the plan, but because of the favor he had found in the eyes of Pharaoh, he was set over all the land of Egypt. Pharaoh even placed his ring of authority on Joseph's hand. At just thirty years of age, abundant favor was shown to Joseph by God through Pharaoh. Only in the throne would Pharaoh be greater than Joseph.

MORE OF GOD'S PURPOSE REVEALED

During the seven-year drought that Joseph had foretold, Joseph's brothers, at the insistence of their father, Jacob, came to Egypt seeking food. When Joseph heard of this, he directed that they be brought to him. Thinking that Joseph was dead, the brothers did not recognize him and had no idea from whom they were requesting assistance. After Joseph had helped them, he sent them away. When they returned to him a second time, Joseph disclosed his identity and forgave them for what they had done to him. Then Joseph received permission (abundant favor) from Pharaoh to bring his father and his brethren and their families to live in the land of Egypt—which they did for over four hundred years.

Do you see God's purpose in granting Joseph abundant favor on each of these occasions and in all that he accomplished? It was through these events that God's chosen people, the children of Israel, became established.

The story also demonstrates just how God might withhold His favor in order to accomplish His greater purpose. Initially, Joseph did not receive God's abundant favor in the eyes of his brothers. If he had, Joseph would be just another name in the Old Testament and God would have had to find other means and other people to carry out His purpose.

CHILDREN OF ISRAEL – ABUNDANT FAVOR

"And the children of Israel were fruitful, and increased abundantly, and multiplied, and waxed exceeding mighty; and the land was filled with them."

(Exodus 1:7)

Yes, the children of Israel multiplied and prospered greatly in the land of Egypt, but things changed. Joseph had died and a new pharaoh came into power, one who knew nothing about Joseph. Because he feared the children of Israel, their vast numbers and their might, the Israelites were forced into slavery where they remained for the balance of their sojourn in Egypt.

"And they made their lives bitter with hard bondage, in mortar and in brick, and in all manner of service in the field: All their service wherein they made them serve, was with rigour." (Exodus 1:14)

"Let My People Go!"

In His timing, God selected Moses and his brother Aaron to appeal to Pharaoh for the release of the Israelites and to lead them into the land that He had promised to the patriarch Abraham. They were instructed to convey to Pharaoh the words of God, *"Let my people go!"* But time after time, Pharaoh refused to obey God's command.

On each occasion that Pharaoh's heart was hardened against God and the children of Israel, God imposed a severe plague or pestilence upon the Egyptians. It was the final plague that forced Pharaoh to surrender—and even *order* the Israelites out of the land. But before this plague, a very unusual thing occurred.

GOD'S ABUNDANT FAVOR BESTOWED

God said to Moses: "Speak now in the ears of the people, and let every man borrow of his [Egyptian] neighbor, and every woman of her [Egyptian] neighbor, jewels of silver and jewels of gold. And the Lord gave the people favor [abundant favor] in the sight of the Egyptians..."   (Exodus 11:2,3)

Picture the scene. Here are the Egyptians who have been slavemasters of the children of Israel for at least two hundred years. At the hands of the God whom these slaves worship, the Egyptians have suffered horrible plagues and pestilences. Unbelievably, in preparation for the escape of the Israelites, the Egyptians are voluntarily agreeing to "lend" them all they need, including their jewels of silver and gold. Is this God-provided abundant favor or what?

When the children of Israel are prepared to leave the country, God brings about the worst and final plague.

"And Moses said, Thus saith the Lord, About midnight will I go out into the midst of Egypt:

And all the firstborn in the land of Egypt shall die, from the firstborn of Pharaoh that sitteth upon his throne, even unto the firstborn of the maidservant that is behind the mill; and all the firstborn of beasts."

(Exodus 11:4,5)

God now bestows even greater abundant favor upon the children of Israel. They are to be spared the horror that the Egyptians must endure.

SPECIAL INSTRUCTIONS, SPECIAL ACTION

In order to protect the Israelites, each home is given special, detailed instructions. They are to kill a male lamb, without blemish and less than a year old, place the blood from the lamb in a basin, and follow these directions:

"And ye shall take a bunch of hyssop, and dip it in the blood that is in the basin, and strike the lintel and two side posts with the blood that is in the basin; and none of you shall go out at the door of his house until the morning.

For the Lord will pass through to smite the Egyptians; and when he seeth the blood upon the lintel, and on the two side posts, the Lord will pass over the door, and will not suffer the destroyer to come in unto your houses or smite you." (Exodus 12:22,23)

THE FINAL PLAGUE

"And it came to pass, that at midnight the Lord smote all the firstborn in the land of Egypt, from the firstborn of Pharaoh who sat on his throne unto the firstborn of the captive that was in the dungeon; and all the firstborn of cattle." (Exodus 12:29)

According to God's promise, not one Israelite was slain this night. God does grant abundant favor and the children of Israel are an outstanding example—even to this day. Starting with Joseph, we see God's purpose in granting *His* favor to him and to the children of Israel. The Lord was preparing His chosen people for entrance into the promised land and to become the source of Human Redemption (Jesus Christ).

ABUNDANT FAVOR OFTEN PROVIDED

If we assume that special biblical emphasis indicates special favor, then there are many more examples of people such as Esther (Esther 2:15,17) Daniel (Daniel 1:9), Hannah (1 Samuel: 1:1-28), and even Jesus (Luke 2:52) who received abundant favor. And of course, there are numerous instances where the specific word *favor* may not be used, but where it is apparent through the use of other words and phrases that the person or people were receiving God's favor.

WHAT ABOUT ASKING

"And this is the confidence that we have in him, that, if we ask anything according to his will, he heareth us:

And if we know that he hears us, whatsoever we ask, we know that we have the petitions that we desired of him." (1 John 5:14,15)

This Scripture, along with many others, answers the "what about asking" question. Each teaches us anew that God is the source of all things good, and by asking we acknowledge that fact.

The Psalmist prayed: "I intreated [asked for] thy favor with my whole heart: be merciful unto me according to thy word" (Psalm 119:58).

And again: "Remember me, O Lord, with thy favor, that thou bearest unto thy people..."
(Psalm 106:4)

Then there are words such as *petition* and *supplication* that indicate something special is being asked of God. But there are other even more familiar passages concerning asking and receiving. Here are three of the most often quoted.

> "And whatsoever ye shall ask in my name, that will I do, that the Father may be glorified in the Son.
> If ye shall ask anything in my name, I will do it." (John 14:13,14) (Jesus speaking)

> "Therefore I say unto you, What things soever ye desire, when ye pray, believe that ye receive them, and ye shall have them". (Mark 11:24)

> "Ye have not because ye ask not."
> (James 4:2b)

BE CAREFUL!

Based on the promises found in the Scriptures, we can have great confidence that God welcomes our asking Him for the right things and for the right reasons. However, there is danger that this confidence can be carried to extremes. We see examples of it on every hand. *Name it and claim it* is flourishing, but are Christians being led astray by false hope?

If we dig deeply enough, we will find that each of the foregoing Scripture passages can be qualified in some way, either by the context in which they are used, other passages of Scripture, or the original language. God does not have an *open season* on everything we desire. He may have much better reasons to withhold the thing we ask for than we have in asking for it.

This does not mean that we should pray without expecting results. If that were true, there would be little reason to pray. But the most important aspect of asking is that we are acknowledging the attributes of God and affirming our total dependence upon Him.

WHO CAN *EXPECTANTLY* PRAY THIS PRAYER

Only those who have accepted Jesus Christ as their personal Savior, have been forgiven of their sins, and are spiritually born anew can confidently and expectantly pray this prayer. They are the children of God and have the privilege to call Him Father. They have inherent favor and can be confident of abundant favor.

The Bible says, *"If I regard iniquity in my heart, the Lord will not hear me"* (Psalm 66:18). Those who have never accepted Christ and received forgiveness of their sins cannot help but have iniquity in their hearts. Iniquity is sin. The Bible says, *"For **all** have sinned, and come short of the glory of God"* (Romans 3:23) (Bold type mine).

It is important to realize that not just unbelievers can have iniquity in their hearts. *Believers* also sin...often...even daily. The difference is

The Prayer for Abundant Favor

that a believer is not under the *control* of sin. The believer does not serve the author of sin (Satan). He serves a risen, living Savior, Jesus the Christ, and obedient believers are under *His* control.

In addition, the believer has access to immediate forgiveness of any sin he does commit. First John 1:9 tells us, *"If we confess our sins, he is faithful and just to forgive us our sins, and to cleanse us from all unrighteousness."* Please note: These words were not written to *unbelievers* by the Apostle John. They were written to *believers* for the express purpose of strengthening their fellowship with God through Christ and that their joy in Christ may be full and complete.

More Evidence

Although God may, out of His common grace, hear and answer the prayer of an unbeliever, it is *only* the believer who has the *assurance* that God always hears and responds.

The Bible says, "Now we know that God heareth not sinners: but if any man be a worshipper of God, and doeth his will, him he heareth." (John 9:31)

The Bible says, "The Lord is far from the wicked [unsaved]: but he heareth the prayer of the righteous." (Proverbs 15:29)

The Bible says, "He that turneth away his ear from hearing the law [those who have rejected Christ], even his prayer shall be an abomination [a thing hated by God]." (Proverbs 28:9)

In light of the Scriptures quoted and the foregoing discussion, it is evident who may pray *The Prayer for Abundant Favor* with confidence and the expectation that it will be answered. It is the *believer*. The only prayer that an unbeliever can be *certain* God will hear and answer is the prayer of repentance and the plea for forgiveness.

THE DOOR IS OPEN

Perhaps you are a person who believes that you can receive forgiveness of your sins in some way other than by asking the Lord Jesus

Christ to forgive you. Perhaps you feel Jesus can be left out of the equation without any commitment to Him whatsoever. Or you might believe that if you are a good person and do more good things than bad and faithfully perform certain rituals, your sins will be overlooked, and when you die you will make it to heaven. You certainly are not alone. That is what many believe.

The question is: "If what you believe were not true, would you want to know it?" Of course you would.

The truth is that sin can be forgiven and salvation obtained only through faith in Jesus Christ—only by accepting Him as the Son of God, the risen Savior, and by confessing our sins and asking His forgiveness. It was Jesus Christ, and no other, who paid the penalty for our sins by shedding His blood on the cross at Calvary.

Jesus said, "I am the way, the truth, and the life: no man cometh unto the Father, but by me."
(John 14:6) (bold type mine)

The Apostle Paul wrote, "For ye are all the children of God by faith in **Christ Jesus**."
(Galatians 3:26) (bold type mine)

The Apostle Peter said, "...For there is none other name [Jesus] under heaven given among men whereby we must be saved." (Acts 4:12)

If you have never with your whole heart confessed your sins to Jesus, asked for His forgiveness, and asked Him to come into your heart and take over your life, perhaps you would like to do so before continuing with this book.

Perhaps Even Now?

THE PRAYER OF FAITH

You may prefer praying your prayer of faith in your own words, or you may be more comfortable repeating this suggested prayer. In either case, if you pray with complete sincerity and from the depths of your heart and mean every word you speak, you will receive the free gift of salvation and eternal spiritual life. You will also be blessed with inherent favor and the confidence to pray expectantly for abundant favor.

"Lord Jesus, I believe that You are the Son of God, that You died on the cross to pay the penalty for my sins with Your own blood.

I believe that You rose from the dead the third day and that You will return again.

Lord Jesus, I know that I am a sinner and I come to You now to ask forgiveness of my sins and to ask You to come into my heart and take over my life. I commit my life to You now."

I prayed this prayer on _____

Signed: _____

45

FOR WHAT
SHOULD I PRAY

There is no limit to the number and kinds of situations in which I might find myself where *God's* abundant favor is desired or even critical. Broadly speaking, I might ask for His favor ...

- In a matter involving just God and me.
- In the eyes of another person.
- When I intercede for someone who also finds themselves in need of God's favor.

Some examples are: Asking God's forgiveness; applying for a job; preparing the heart of a person to whom I will be sharing my faith; a personal interview; a pay raise; admission to a college; meetings with boards or committees; reaching an agreement with my spouse; a sales presentation; obtaining a loan. The list could go on and on even down to something as mundane as obtaining a parking place (I speak from experience)!

Nearly everything that affects our lives involves other people. In most cases we will be asking God to grant us abundant favor in the eyes of one person or individuals within a group. However, when we intercede for others we will be asking God to grant *them* favor in the eyes of another person or other people.

Take the case of Donna who had suffered from bone deterioration in her face. Two surgeries had been performed with the purpose of the second to implant a plastic substance to replace bone. However, as time went on, complications developed and the material caused extremely painful infections. It was imperative that additional surgery be performed at a cost of more than seven thousand dollars. Donna did not have the money and the insurance company would no longer cover the surgery. An appeal to the insurance company was to be made by her physician.

Donna was desperately in need of God granting her abundant favor with whoever would make the final decision. Their goodwill was certainly needed! Normally, the chances for a favorable outcome would be slim. To her knowledge, in similar circumstances the company had never changed their initial ruling. Among the many prayers offered on Donna's behalf were those of our Adult Bible Fellowship. We prayed and God answered, not just our prayers, but all who prayed! The insurance company acquiesced! The surgery was successfully performed! Praise God, Donna's need was met. Special favor was granted.

It's important to realize that no matter what words were used, whether specifically for favor or not, in actuality we were all asking God to grant Donna favor in the eyes of the people at the insurance company.

So what are the criteria we may use to determine the things for which we can pray and the things for which we should not pray?

GOD'S WILL

"And this is the confidence that we have in him, that, if we ask anything **according to his will**, he heareth us." (1 John 5:14) (Bold type mine)

We know that not just our prayers for favor but all our requests should be made according to *God's will*. His will, not ours, should always come first and be the main focus of our prayers and our decisions. Even the Son of God was an example of a person who put God's will before His own. (*See* Matthew 26:36-41.)

But we can't just leave it there. One of the questions most frequently asked of pastors and counselors is, *"How can I really know God's will?"* Many books have been written on this subject and there is little we can add to what is available from other sources. However, as God's will pertains to *The Prayer for Abundant Favor*, there are several thoughts that can be helpful.

There are at least three ways in which we can determine whether or not the thing we propose to pray about is in God's will or contrary to it:

- We can search His Word (the Bible).
- We can pray for God's will to be revealed to us by the Holy Spirit.
- We can use sound *spiritual* logic and *spiritual* common sense.

Despite the fact that God reveals His will in many ways, it often seems less difficult to identify what is NOT God's will. Here's an example that was recently brought to my attention by a close friend who for some time has been successfully involved in praying for abundant favor.

It seemed his son had not applied himself very diligently to his college studies this year. It was exam time and my friend was justly concerned. As he knelt to pray that God would give his son favor in the eyes of his professors, he heard a still small voice (the Holy Spirit) within him and he began to apply *spiritual* logic and common sense as he asked himself, "Should I be praying like this?" Because of his son's lack of effort, the answer to his question was obvious. We mutually agreed that a more appropriate prayer might be for "fairness" on the part of the professor—no special favor, just fairness.

FOR HIS NAME'S SAKE

"He restoreth my soul: He leadeth me in the paths of righteousness for His name's sake."

(Psalm 23:3)

Is what I'm asking for protecting the *name* and *reputation* of God? Am I as a Christian requesting anything that would in any way cast a poor reflection on His kingdom, or will it edify the name and work of the Lord?

As chosen representatives for God, it is important that all we say and all we do will magnify His holy name. Our needs and desires are secondary to our responsibilities to Him.

LUST NOT...WANT NOT

"Ye ask and receive not, because ye ask am-iss, that ye may consume it upon your lusts."
(James 4:3)

Remember what we suggested concerning scriptural promises being qualified? Here is the qualifier for James 4:2(b) which told us that we have not because we ask not. The statement speaks for itself. If we are praying for special favor to acquire something that will only satisfy our *lust*, we probably won't receive what we would consider a satisfactory answer. Brother James is very explicit about that!

The word *lust* is most often construed to mean *sexual lust*, which of course is one of its meanings. But *lust* means a strong desire for anything. We can *lust* for money, or a new car, or power, or recognition or many other things of a human nature. We can yearn and even ache for heavenly things, but we usually *lust* for earthly things.

52

MANIPULATION

How easy it can become to use any kind of knowledge or expertise as a means of manipulating another person for our own selfish desires! We need to be constantly on guard against the temptation to do so. Rest assured, others will be greatly influenced by your prayer for abundant favor, but it should always be prayed for the mutual benefit of all those involved.

Many times we don't just stop with trying to manipulate people. We also try to manipulate God. How often have I promised Him that if He will just answer my request, "I'll never do it again!" or "I'll do whatever You want?" Unless our promises truly come from the heart, that is manipulation. Any such attempt is futile. It never works. God cannot be manipulated. He's more than one step ahead of us at all times and He sees through our feeble attempts to influence Him in this way.

THE INTERCEDING PRAYER WARRIOR

From my own twenty years of praying for favor and from the reports of others, I am personally convinced that this prayer can drastically improve your prayer life and your attitude toward prayer.

As you experience answers to your prayers for favor and see God at work, it's amazing what happens to your confidence in all prayer. I know that for me, when I pray *The Prayer for Abundant Favor*, there is an unusually strong sense of assurance that God hears and will respond. This has reflected itself in my prayer life generally. They say that prayer changes things. The thing that prayer has the potential of changing the most is the person who prays.

This prayer can also be the means of you becoming the interceding prayer warrior that God would have you to be. As you will learn, God will fill your heart with the desire to spend most of your prayer time in praying for the benefit of others. Just as Christ now sits at the right hand of God interceding for us (Romans 8:34), so should we be in the business of intercessory prayer for others.

What Christendom needs today are more fighting men and women, more warriors who are willing to use the immeasurable power of prayer as their weapon.

Our war is against Satan and the forces of evil. There are untold numbers who need our help in their fight against these enemies. And we need not be alone in our efforts. There are other Christians who, if asked, will join with us in praying for the needs of others. Group prayer certainly multiplies the weapons and increases the power. It brings even greater results. An army of many is much more effective than a lone combatant.

HOW SHOULD I PRAY?

When Jesus taught His disciples what is known as the *Lord's Prayer*, He was not saying that was to be their only prayer repeated word for word each time they prayed. Although we should use it often, it serves as a pattern or model for prayer. Jesus said, "After this *manner* therefore, pray ye." He did not say, *"Pray these exact words."*

In describing how we pray *The Prayer for Abundant Favor*, may I suggest a pattern or model with which I believe you will be comfortable? How you pray personally will be directed by the Holy Spirit.

THE ESSENTIAL ELEMENTS

As we discuss the essential elements of *The Prayer for Abundant Favor*, we will be using an intercessory prayer similar to one that was prayed about fifteen years ago. Bob and his wife,

Marlene, were preparing to serve as missionaries to the Cree Indians in Alberta, Canada. Their time for departure was drawing near but they had no visa and no assurance that one would even be issued. They needed abundant favor with the Canadian authorities.

Here, then, are the essential elements of *The Prayer for Abundant Favor*:

I. SELF-CLEANSING

"If I regard iniquity in my heart, the Lord will not hear me." Psalm 66:18

"If we confess our sins, he is faithful and just to forgive us our sins and to cleanse us from all unrighteousness." 1 John 1:9

Anytime that we kneel before the throne of grace, whether praying *The Prayer for Abundant Favor* or any other prayer, we must do so cleansed from all sin and unrighteousness. It is the only way we can be sure God will hear us. But of much greater importance than our being heard is His majestic holiness. Because of this holiness, God will never allow us to carry sin into His awesome presence, nor will He hear us if we attempt to do so. Therefore, the first element of this or any prayer should be the confession of any known or unknown sins, whether sins of commission or omission, and the plea for forgiveness. As we said before, 1 John 1:9 assures us that our request will be granted.

Example: *"Dear Lord, as I come to You today on behalf of Bob and Marlene, I want to enter into Your presence free from any sin. Please forgive me for the way I talked to my friend yesterday and for being angry with the guy who was tailgating me. Please forgive me for the thoughts I had toward the neighbor and for anything I have said or done which was not pleasing to You. Please forgive me also for any sin I may not realize I have committed."*

II. SEVENTY TIMES SEVEN

When the Apostle Peter came to Jesus (Matthew 18:21,22) and asked if he forgave someone seven times would that be enough, Jesus replied, "*I say not unto thee, Until seven times: but, Until seventy times seven*" (Matthew 18:22).

The first element of our prayer for abundant favor was *Self-Cleansing*—seeking God's forgiveness of any sins we have committed. But in order to be spiritually cleansed, we must consider the vital second element. Let's see what Jesus has to say about it.

"For if ye forgive men their trespasses, your heavenly Father will also forgive you:
But if ye forgive not men their trespasses, neither will your Father forgive your trespasses."

(Matthew 6:14,15)

One of the greatest deterrents to an effective prayer life is a spirit of unforgiveness or bitterness toward another person. Unquestionably, we should include forgiving others as an element in *The Prayer for Abundant Favor*. It seems that one of the reasons God wants us to forgive others is so He can forgive us.

Example: *"Lord, I have failed to forgive my friend* _____ *for what she did to me. It has eaten and eaten at me and has been a barrier to my relationship with You. I want to forgive her now. I want to release this matter to You. It is in Your hands. I am now free of it. Thank You, Lord."*

Warning! It is dangerous to profess forgiveness of someone when it is not done sincerely and from the heart. It is speaking idle words, an affront to God, and an attempt to manipulate Him for our own purposes. He will not respond kindly to it.

The *"Seventy Times Seven"* element very likely will be the one many people will have the most difficulty with initially. Forgiving someone who has seriously harmed you may not be easy, but it is what God requires of us.

A great way to forgive a person is to first ask for *their* forgiveness. Sound strange? Listen!

After hearing an excellent sermon on forgiveness and being convicted by it, I went to a friend who had seriously wronged me in a business matter and repeated the words the pastor had recommended: "I've come here today to ask your forgiveness. Since our misunderstanding, I have been angry with you and have had bitterness in my heart toward you. Will you please forgive me?"

Immediately the burden was lifted and the relationship was restored. Even though what *he* had done and the fact that *he* had never sought *my* forgiveness was never mentioned, *my* asking *him* for *his* forgiveness of *me* was in itself an act of forgiving *him*.

Why should I have asked my friend for *his* forgiveness when *he* was the one who was at fault? The answer! If damaged relationships between two people are ever to be repaired, someone has to go first—and the one who does receives the greater blessing. The Bible never mentions which person should forgive first. It just says *forgive*!

Of all six elements, this could well be the most essential. When combined with the first element, we are free to openly and guiltlessly communicate with our Lord.

It was a startling revelation to me when I first noticed where in relationship to the teachings of Christ the verses we quoted are located. They are found *immediately after the Lord's Prayer.* How profound!

Here Jesus has just given His model for prayer, the ramifications of which are endless, and He sums it up by telling us if we do not forgive others, we will not be forgiven. Again; how profound!

III. OUR NEED DEFINED

If we have asked forgiveness for our own sins and have forgiven those who have wronged us, we are now ready to define the need. Although God knows our needs even before we ask

Him, it seems that He would prefer hearing about them from our own lips—and as specifically as possible.

One woman tells me that she believes so much in being specific in her prayers that when she prays for rain, she gives the Lord her address. We needn't go quite that far, but we do want to adequately describe the need.

Example: *"Lord, You have called Bob and Marlene to be Your missionaries to the Cree Indians in Canada. I humbly bring before You the problem they are having in obtaining a visa. They are not certain they will receive one or how soon it might be. They are ready to leave now, but without the visa, they will be unable to go."*

IV. LOVE THY NEIGHBOR AS THYSELF

Before continuing in a prayer for abundant favor, I believe it is most important to establish a love relationship among the parties involved. Even though we may not personally know every individual, we can still express love for

them, God's love and our love. But again, it must
be sincere and from the heart. It is done not to
attempt to manipulate God, but because we are
instructed to *love our neighbors.* Furthermore,
nothing in this world can withstand the power of
love whether it be bestowed by God directly or
channeled through one of His children.

First, we affirm God's love for each person involved and then we express our own love
for each person. It's amazing when we pray like
this how the Holy Spirit confirms the love relationship which He establishes.

Example: *"Lord,before requesting Your
favor, I want to affirm Your love for the official in
Canada who will make the decision to issue the visa
for Bob and Marlene. I also want to sincerely confess
my love for him and to ask Your blessing upon him.*

*I pray that You will crown him with loving-
kindness and tender mercy. I pray, Lord, that his
needs will be met and that You will prosper him both
materially and spiritually. I pray for good health for
him and for his family. And Lord, if he does not know*

You, I pray that You will draw him to You.

V. THE PETITION

Example: *"Lord, In the name of Jesus, I ask You now to grant both Bob and Marlene Your abundant favor in the eyes of the Canadian official. I pray that through You, they will meet with his goodwill and the visa will be issued promptly."*

Note: If we pray in the authority of the name of Jesus, we are demonstrating our trust in His promise that if we ask anything in His name, He will do it so that the Father may be glorified in the Son *(See* John 14:13,14).

VI. THANK YOU, LORD

Example: *"Lord, I thank You for the opportunity You have given me to intercede for Bob and Marlene. I thank You for hearing my plea for Your abundant favor, and I humbly thank You for whatever answer You give. I praise You, O Lord."*

God graciously and promptly answered the intercessory prayer for Bob and Marlene. He granted them abundant favor in the eyes of the

Canadian official and the visa was received within two weeks.

SUMMARY OF ELEMENTS

Let's review the prayer as it would be prayed in its entirety:

SELF-CLEANSING. Confess to God the sins of your heart and ask Him to forgive you.

SEVENTY TIMES SEVEN. Forgive others of any and all wrongdoing, just as God has forgiven you.

OUR NEED DEFINED. Tell God your specific needs.

LOVE THY NEIGHBOR AS THYSELF. Affirm God's love and your love for those individuals who have needs as well as those whose favor you are seeking.

THE PETITION. Ask God, in the name of Jesus, to grant your request for abundant favor.

THANK YOU, LORD. Thank Him! Praise Him!

CONCLUSION

As stated before, *The Prayer for Abundant Favor* is a pattern or model that has been developed and proven over time. Variations have been used and God has graciously answered. Many have been blessed. Many have learned anew the value of prayer and have gained new confidence that God *does* hear His children and *does* respond.

It is impossible to recount all the occasions when God has answered prayers for abundant favor during the last twenty plus years. They are numerous, and some are even miraculous. We have an awesome God who takes great joy in the prayerful trust of His children. He wants us to carry *everything* to Him in prayer. As a matter of fact, our prayers are a sweet aroma to our Lord.

"Let my prayer be set forth before thee as incense; and the lifting up of my hands as the evening sacrifice." (Psalm 114:2)

The words which we speak in prayer in and of themselves do not produce abundant favor, but it is *through* prayer that God bestows this precious gift upon us. May He richly bless you as you experience your amazing answers to:

The Prayer for Abundant Favor.

PART II

MY
ABUNDANT FAVOR
PRAYER DIARY

As we look back, we often wish we had kept a written record of many of the events in our lives—like answered prayer. The next few pages are designed for that purpose. Simply write the details of your *Prayers for Abundant Favor* and the answers to them.

Now when *you* look back, you'll be more than pleased and amazed at God's willingness to to answer when He hears your voice.

My Abundant Favor Prayer Diary

DATE _____

♦ SINS I CONFESS THIS DAY

_____

_____

♦ PERSON I FORGIVE THIS DAY

_____

♦ THE NEED DEFINED

_____

_____

♦ I AFFIRM GOD'S LOVE AND MY LOVE FOR

_____

_____

♦ MY PETITION TO GOD

♦ MY THANKS TO GOD

♦ GOD'S ANSWER _____

_____

_____

DATE _____

71

My Abundant Favor Prayer Diary

DATE _____

♦ SINS I CONFESS THIS DAY

_____

_____

♦ PERSON I FORGIVE THIS DAY

_____

♦ THE NEED DEFINED

_____

_____

♦ I AFFIRM GOD'S LOVE AND MY LOVE FOR

_____

_____

♦ MY PETITION TO GOD

♦ MY THANKS TO GOD

♦ GOD'S ANSWER _____

_____

_____

DATE _____

72

My Abundant Favor Prayer Diary

DATE _____

♦ SINS I CONFESS THIS DAY

_____

_____

♦ PERSON I FORGIVE THIS DAY

_____

♦ THE NEED DEFINED

_____

_____

♦ I AFFIRM GOD'S LOVE AND MY LOVE FOR

_____

_____

♦ MY PETITION TO GOD

♦ MY THANKS TO GOD

♦ GOD'S ANSWER _____

_____

_____

DATE _____

My Abundant Favor Prayer Diary

DATE _____

◆ SINS I CONFESS THIS DAY

_____
_____

◆ PERSON I FORGIVE THIS DAY

_____

◆ THE NEED DEFINED

_____
_____

◆ I AFFIRM GOD'S LOVE AND MY LOVE FOR

_____
_____

◆ MY PETITION TO GOD

◆ MY THANKS TO GOD

◆ GOD'S ANSWER _____

_____
_____

DATE _____

My Abundant Favor Prayer Diary

DATE _____

- ◆ SINS I CONFESS THIS DAY

_____
_____

- ◆ PERSON I FORGIVE THIS DAY

_____

- ◆ THE NEED DEFINED

_____
_____

- ◆ I AFFIRM GOD'S LOVE AND MY LOVE FOR

_____
_____

- ◆ MY PETITION TO GOD

- ◆ MY THANKS TO GOD

- ◆ GOD'S ANSWER _____

_____
_____

DATE _____

My Abundant Favor Prayer Diary

DATE _____

♦ SINS I CONFESS THIS DAY

_____

_____

♦ PERSON I FORGIVE THIS DAY

_____

♦ THE NEED DEFINED

_____

_____

♦ I AFFIRM GOD'S LOVE AND MY LOVE FOR

_____

_____

♦ MY PETITION TO GOD

♦ MY THANKS TO GOD

♦ GOD'S ANSWER _____

_____

_____

DATE _____

PART III

FERVENT PRAYER

AVAILETH MUCH

"THE EFFECTUAL FERVENT PRAYER OF A RIGHTEOUS MAN AVAILETH MUCH."
JAMES 5:16

"The neglect of prayer is a grand hindrance to holiness. 'We have not because we ask not.' Oh, how meek and gentle, how lowly in heart, how full of love both to God and to man, might you have been at this day, if you had only asked! If you had continued instant in prayer!

Ask, that you may thoroughly experience and perfectly practice the whole of that religion which our Lord has so beautifully described in the Sermon on the Mount." JOHN WESLEY

For the eyes of the Lord are over the righteous, and his ears are open unto their prayers...

1 PETER 3:12

Continue in prayer, and watch in the same with thanksgiving. COLOSSIANS 4:2

Pray without ceasing. 1 THESSALONIANS 5:17

———————

I will therefore that men pray every where, lifting up holy hands, without wrath and doubting. 1 TIMOTHY 2:8

———————

Ask, and it shall be given you; seek, and ye shall find; knock, and it shall be opened unto you.
MATTHEW 7:7

———————

Be careful [anxious] for nothing; but in every thing by prayer and supplication with thanksgiving let your requests be made known unto God.
PHILIPPIANS 4:6

———————

Again I say unto you, That if two of you shall agree on earth as touching any thing that they shall ask, it shall be done for them of my Father which is in heaven. MATTHEW 18:19

"Prayer should be the breath of our breathing, the thought of our thinking, the soul of our feeling, and the life of our living, the sound of our hearing, the growth of our growing.

Prayer in its magnitude is length without end, width without bounds, height without top, and depth without bottom. Illimitable in its breadth, exhaustless in height, fathomless in depths and infinite in extension." HOMER W. HODGE

For this cause we also, since the day we heard it, do not cease to pray for you, and to desire that ye might be filled with the knowledge of his will in all wisdom and spiritual understanding.

COLOSSIANS 1:9

Ye have not chosen me, but I have chosen you, and ordained you, that ye should go and bring forth fruit, and that your fruit should remain: that whatsoever ye shall ask of the Father in my name, he may give it you. JOHN 15:16

Verily, verily, I say unto you, He that believeth on me, the works that I do shall he do also; and greater works than these shall he do; because I go unto my Father. JOHN 14:12

―――――――――

And whatsoever ye shall ask in my name, that will I do, that the Father may be glorified in the Son.

If ye shall ask any thing in my name, I will do it. JOHN 14:13,14

―――――――――

Jesus answered and said unto them, Verily I say unto you, If ye have faith, and doubt not, ye shall not only do this which is done to the fig tree, but also if ye shall say unto this mountain, Be thou removed, and be thou cast into the sea; it shall be done.

And all things, whatsoever ye shall ask in prayer, believing, ye shall receive.

MATTHEW 21:21,22

"Prayer is no petty duty, put into a corner; no piecemeal performance made out of the fragments of time which have been snatched from business and other engagements of life; but it means that the best of our time, the heart of our time and strength must be given."

E.M. BOUNDS

———————

But we will give ourselves continually to prayer, and to the ministry of the word. ACTS 6:4

———————

And in that day ye shall ask me nothing. Verily, verily, I say unto you, Whatsoever ye shall ask the Father in my name, he will give it you.

Hitherto have ye asked nothing in my name: ask, and ye shall receive, that your joy may be full. JOHN 16:23,24

———————

The LORD is far from the wicked: but he heareth the prayer of the righteous. PROVERBS 15:29

"He who has the spirit of prayer has the highest interest in the court of heaven. And the only way to retain it is to keep it in constant employment.

Apostasy begins in the closet. No man ever backslid from the life and power of Christianity who continued constant and fervent in private prayer.

He who prays without ceasing is likely to rejoice evermore." ADAM CLARKE

If ye abide in me, and my words abide in you, ye shall ask what ye will, and it shall be done unto you. JOHN 15:7

Ye have heard that it hath been said, Thou shalt love thy neighbour, and hate thine enemy.

But I say unto you, Love your enemies, bless them that curse you, do good to them that hate you, and pray for them which despitefully use you, and persecute you. MATTHEW 5:43,44

Wherefore take unto you the whole armour of God, that ye may be able to withstand in the evil day, and having done all, to stand.

Stand therefore, having your loins girt about with truth, and having on the breastplate of righteousness;

And your feet shod with the preparation of the gospel of peace;

Above all, taking the shield of faith, wherewith ye shall be able to quench all the fiery darts of the wicked.

And take the helmet of salvation, and the sword of the Spirit, which is the word of God:

Praying always with all prayer and supplication in the Spirit, and watching thereunto with all perseverance and supplication for all saints. EPHESIANS 6:13-18

———————

But know that the LORD hath set apart him that is godly for himself: the LORD will hear when I call unto him. PSALM 4:3

"Get into the real work of intercession, and remember, it is a work, a work that taxes every
power; but a work which has no snare. Intercession is a hidden ministry which brings forth
fruit whereby the Father is glorified."

OSWALD CHAMBERS

If my people, which are called by my name,
shall humble themselves, and pray, and seek My
face, and turn from their wicked ways; then will I
hear from heaven, and will forgive their sin, and
will heal their land. 2 CHRONICLES 7:14

Now when Daniel knew that the writing was
signed, he went into his house; and his windows
being open in his chamber toward Jerusalem, he
kneeled upon his knees three times a day, and
prayed, and gave thanks before his God, as he did
aforetime. DANIEL 6:10

My voice shalt thou hear in the morning, O LORD; in the morning will I direct my prayer unto thee, and will look up.   PSALM 5:3

_____

Evening, and morning, and at noon, will I pray, and cry aloud: and he shall hear my voice.

PSALM 55:17

_____

And he spake a parable unto them to this end, that men ought to pray, and not to faint.   LUKE 18:1

_____

"You need not utterly despair even of those who for the present 'turn again and rend you.' For if all your arguments and persuasives fail, there is yet another remedy left, and one that is frequently found effectual, when no other method avails. This is prayer.

Therefore, whatsoever you desire or want, either for others or for your own soul, Ask, and it shall be given you."   JOHN WESLEY

The man answered and said unto them, Why herein is a marvellous thing, that ye know not from whence he is, and yet he hath opened mine eyes.

Now we know that God heareth not sinners: but if any man be a worshipper of God, and doeth his will, him he heareth.   JOHN 9:30,31

———————

And when he had taken the book, the four beasts and four and twenty elders fell down before the Lamb, having every one of them harps, and golden vials full of odours, which are the prayers of saints.   REVELATION 5:8

———————

Is any sick among you? let him call for the elders of the church; and let them pray over him, anointing him with oil in the name of the Lord:

And the prayer of faith shall save the sick, and the Lord shall raise him up; and if he have committed sins, they shall be forgiven him.

JAMES 5:14,15

"In fact, it [prayer] works so well by apparent ac-
cident, it's puzzling that more don't bother to find
out how it works in actuality. It works so well in a
crisis, one wonders why we don't implement it on
a regular basis." JACK W. HAYFORD

———————

And when he looked on him, he was afraid,
and said, What is it, Lord? And he said unto him,
Thy prayers and thine alms are come up for a me-
morial before God. ACTS 10:4

———————

Let my prayer be set forth before thee as
incense; and the lifting up of my hands as the evening sacrifice. PSALM 141:2

———————

Watch ye therefore, and pray always, that
ye may be accounted worthy to escape all these
things that shall come to pass, and to stand before the Son of man. LUKE 21:36

Humble yourselves in the sight of the Lord, and he shall lift you up. JAMES 4:10

Likewise the Spirit also helpeth our infirmities: for we know not what we should pray for as we ought: but the Spirit itself maketh intercession for us with groanings which cannot be uttered. ROMANS 8:26

"The real business of your life as a saved soul is intercessory prayer. Wherever God puts you in circumstances, pray immediately. Pray that His atonement may be realized in other lives as it has been in yours. Pray for your friends now; pray for those with whom you come in contact now."

OSWALD CHAMBERS

If any of you lack wisdom, let him ask of God, that giveth to all men liberally, and upbraideth not; and it shall be given him. JAMES 1:5

And another angel came and stood at the altar, having a golden censer; and there was given unto him much incense, that he should offer it with the prayers of all saints upon the golden altar which was before the throne.

And the smoke of the incense, which came with the prayers of the saints, ascended up before God out of the angel's hand.

REVELATION 8:3,4

Because thy lovingkindness is better than life, my lips shall praise thee.

Thus will I bless thee while I live: I will lift up my hands in thy name.

My soul shall be satisfied as with marrow and fatness; and my mouth shall praise thee with joyful lips: When I remember thee upon my bed, and meditate on thee in the night watches.

PSALM 63:3-6

"The particular value of private prayer consists in being able to approach God with more freedom, and unbosom ourselves more fully than in any other way. Between us and God there are private and personal interests, sins to confess and wants to be supplied, which it would be improper to disclose to the world. This duty is enforced by the example of good men in all ages."

AMOS BINNEY

And it came to pass in those days, that he [Jesus] went out into a mountain to pray, and continued all night in prayer to God. LUKE 6:12

Be kindly affectioned one to another with brotherly love; in honour preferring one another;

Not slothful in business; fervent in spirit; serving the Lord;

Rejoicing in hope; patient in tribulation; continuing instant in prayer. ROMANS 12:10-12

"The one concern of the devil is to keep the saints from praying. He fears nothing from prayerless studies, prayerless work, prayerless religion. He laughs at our toil, mocks at our wisdom, but trembles when we pray." SAMUEL CHADWICK

"Become an intercessor, and you will experience for the first time the blessedness of prayer as you find out that God will make use of you to share His blessings with others through prayer. You will find that He from heaven will do things in answer to your prayers which otherwise would not have been done." ANDREW MURRAY

"Prayer is able to prevail with heaven and bow omnipotence to its desire."

CHARLES HADDEN SPURGEON

ABOUT THE AUTHOR

Clarence L. Blasier is a resident of North Canton, Ohio. He is a charter member of The Chapel in North Canton and is active in evangelism training and other ministries.

Blasier is founder and president of Bethesda Outreach Ministries which offers financial assistance to low income families.

He has an extensive business and public service background and has held prominent local, state, and national civic organization offices.

OTHER BOOKS BY CLARENCE L. BLASIER

Bible Answers for Every Need

What To Believe and Why

*May I Share Something With You
Someone Once Shared With Me?*

Live in Victory

The Golden Treasury of Bible Wisdom